Almost Late
to School
And More School

written by
Carol Diggory Shields

illustrated by
Paul Meisel

PUFFIN BOOKS

For Melody, a friend like that
—C.D.S.

For Barb, Bern, Peter, Ted, and Louisa
—P.M.

PUFFIN BOOKS
Published by the Penguin Group
Penguin Young Readers Group, 345 Hudson Street, New York, New York 10014, U.S.A.
Penguin Group (Canada), 10 Alcorn Avenue, Toronto, Ontario, Canada M4V 3B2 (a division of Pearson Penguin Canada Inc.)
Penguin Books Ltd, 80 Strand, London WC2R 0RL, England
Penguin Ireland, 25 St Stephen's Green, Dublin 2, Ireland (a division of Penguin Books Ltd)
Penguin Group (Australia), 250 Camberwell Road, Camberwell, Victoria 3124, Australia (a division of Pearson Australia Group Pty Ltd)
Penguin Books India Pvt Ltd, 11 Community Centre, Panchsheel Park, New Delhi - 110 017, India
Penguin Group (NZ), Cnr Airborne and Rosedale Roads, Albany, Auckland, New Zealand (a division of Pearson New Zealand Ltd)
Penguin Books (South Africa) (Pty) Ltd, 24 Sturdee Avenue, Rosebank, Johannesburg 2196, South Africa

Registered Offices: Penguin Books Ltd, 80 Strand, London WC2R 0RL, England

First published in the United States of America by Dutton Children's Books, a division of Penguin Putnam Books for Young Readers, 2003
Published by Puffin Books, a division of Penguin Young Readers Group, 2005

1 3 5 7 9 10 8 6 4 2

Text copyright © Carol Diggory Shields, 2003
Illustrations copyright © Paul Meisel, 2003
All rights reserved

CIP Data is available.

Puffin Books ISBN 0-14-240328-8

Manufactured in China

Contents

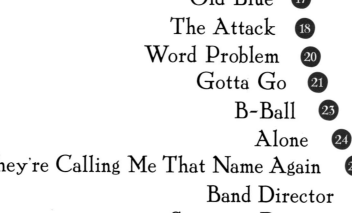

First Day

Thank you for showing me
This very nice school.
The cubbies are nice,
And the easels are cool.
The blocks look like fun,
And the chairs are just right.
The hamster is cute,
And you say he won't bite.
The playground has sand
And seesaws and swings,
And the dress-up corner
Is full of neat things.
The posters are pretty
That show ABC's.
Too bad I can't stay.
Could you call my mom, please?

4

Almost Late

First there was a landslide
That completely blocked the street.

And then I stepped in quicksand—
I could hardly move my feet!

Then I had to help this kid
To get his lunch box back
From a pack of hungry poodles
That was ready to attack.

6

I was almost at the schoolyard—
Just one block away—
When a nice old lady asked me
If I'd help her find her way.
And then...

It's only 8:15?
I got here right on time?
Nope. No problems getting here.
My walk to school was fine.

Jilly's Jealous of Jana

Jilly's Jealous of Jana.
Jana wins every race,
And she doesn't have stupid freckles
Freckled all over her face.

Jana's jealous of Ellie,
'Cause Ellie jumps rope the best,
And Ellie gets extra credit
On every arithmetic test.

Ellie's jealous of Amber.
Amber is so good at art,
The teacher always asks Amber
To color the posters and charts.

Amber is jealous of Jilly.
Jilly dances ballet on her toes,
And Jilly has cute little freckles
Sprinkled across her nose.

Science Fair Project

PURPOSE:
The purpose of my project this year
Is to make my brother disappear.

HYPOTHESIS:
The world would be a better place
If my brother vanished without a trace.

MATERIALS:
3 erasers
White-out
Disappearing ink
1 younger brother
1 kitchen sink

PROCEDURE:
Chop up the erasers.
Add the white-out and the ink.
Rub it on the brother
While he's standing in the sink.

RESULTS:
The kid was disappearing!
I had almost proved my theorem!
When all at once my mom came home
And made me re-appear him.

CONCLUSION:
Experiment a failure.
My brother is still here.
But I'm already planning
For the science fair *next* year.

Oral Report

These are the things that will happen
When I stand up to give my report:

    1. I'll trip on my way to the front of the class.

    2. My voice
will come out as a snort.

    3. My buttons
will all come unbuttoned.

4. My face
will turn red as a rose.

5. I'll forget
just how to speak English.

6. Stuff will come out of my nose.

7. My index cards
will be upside down.

8. My mind
will go totally numb.

9. My knees
will knock together.

10. The whole class will know that I'm dumb.

My oral report is finished!
Looks like I actually survived.
I might even get up and do it again
In the year three thousand and five.

Show and Share

I brought my snake to school today. The teacher said it was okay—as long as he was safe and sound and not out wriggling all around. I put him carefully inside a sturdy bag so he could hide and not be nervous or freaked out

as I carried him about. And everything was going fine, until it came to sharing time. "Here is my snake!" I proudly said—and pulled out my dad's lunch instead!

Shannon

Shannon is shy.
She's like my cousin's cat.
If you try to catch her,
She runs away—*scat!*

But if you're sitting quietly,
Holding very still,
That cat will come and sit by you,
Just like Shannon will.

Old Blue

I've been lost, tossed,
And flung around.
Still...
I've hung around.

You sat on me,
Fell flat on me.
I kept your place,
Played first base.

Held inside
What you wanted to hide
(Moldy old sandwiches,
That note from a girl).

But now...
I'm worn, torn,
Tattered and battered,
Losing my grip,
And my zippers won't zip.

Guess it's off to Goodwill.
I'm just hoping still
You'll sometimes think back
To this old blue backpack.

The Attack

Wendy started wriggling,
  Which started Stevie giggling.
    The giggles spread to Shawna,
      Then to Tammy, Tim, and Tru.

The teacher made a frowny face,
  Which made the giggles jump on Grace,
    Then Gracie passed those giggles on
      To Kyle and Mary Lou.

The teacher said, "Now quiet down!"
The giggles grabbed poor Chelsea Brown,
Who gave them quick to Nicky,
    Who shared with Ben and Drew.

The teacher said, "What's going on?"
The giggles hopped from Drew to Juan.
Juan passed them on to Abraham,
    Who gave them to both Sues.

Those giggles kept on going—
They never did stop growing—
Until they tickled Teacher
    And made her giggle, too.

Word Problem

If a train leaves the station at half past two,
Going fifty miles an hour toward Kalamazoo,
And Kevin the conductor has three quarters and a dime,
And Anna has bananas but really needs a lime,
And Anna sells bananas for forty cents a bunch,
How many minutes do we have till lunch?

Gotta Go

Gotta go, gotta go,
Really, really gotta go.
Should have gone long ago,
Yes, I know, yes, I know.
But now I really,
Really gotta go.

But my teacher's Mrs. Dean,
And she's strict and kind of mean,
And I hate to raise my hand,
'Cause she doesn't understand
That I really, really,
Really gotta go.

So I'm sitting here a-wiggling.
My legs are jumpy-jiggling.
I'm praying for that bell to ring,
When I will run like anything,
'Cause I really, really,
REALLY gotta go!

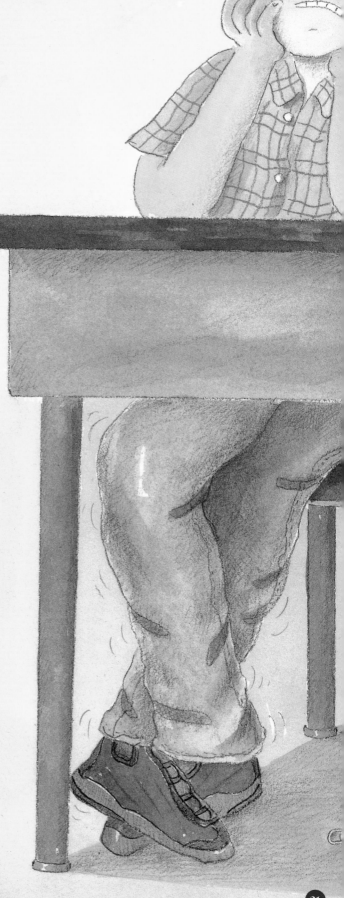

B-Ball

Rebound,
Swish sound.
Bounce, pass,
Break fast.
Three in the key,
Over to me.
Hook shot,
I'm hot.
Back court,
Shoot short.
Round the rim,
Almost in.
Free throw,
Way to go!
We won,
Had fun.

Alone

In the middle of this riot,
I'd like to find a place that's quiet.
A little space that's shaped like me.
A little place where I can be
alone.

They're Calling Me That Name Again

They're calling me that name again—
It's driving me insane—
In voices shrill, like little drills,
Attacking my poor brain.
In classroom, playground, hall, and gym,
From swing and slide and bleacher,
I hear it everywhere I go—
"Teacher! Teacher! Teacher!"

Band Director

Our band director used to be real mean.
Our band director used to shout and scream.
Our band director used to be all grumpy.
Our band director said we made him jumpy.

But *now*,
Our band director is as calm as a clam.
Our band director is as gentle as a lamb.
Our band director gives us smiles and hugs.
Our band director is wearing earplugs.

Sitting in Detention

I'm sitting in detention,
And I feel like I've been framed.
Sitting in detention,
I'm the one who got the blame.

Sitting in the classroom,
I was doing nothing wrong.
The girl who's on my right
Asked me to pass a note along.

I was doing her a favor,
Being helpful as could be.
I was passing it along
When the teacher looked at me.

She made me stand and open it
And read it then and there.
The note said something not so nice
About the teacher's hair.

So I'm sitting in detention,
Just waiting out the time—
Sitting in detention
For a crime that was not mine.

Jump Rope Rhyme

I'm a little schoolgirl,
Dressed in pink.
At jumping rope
I really stink.

I jump in, and
One—two—three,
I fall right down
And skin my knee.

Jump on one foot,
Jump on two.
The rope gets tangled
Around my shoe.

As a jump-rope jumper,
I have no hope.
But I'm very, very good
At turning this rope!

Fund-raiser

We're having a bake sale, we're having a cake sale.
We're selling you candy and magnets and bows.
We're raffling chances on moonlight romances
And TVs and CDs and school-logo clothes.

We're walking for new bats, we're jogging for gym mats.
We're selling subscriptions to buy uniforms.
The art room needs paint sets, the band needs new clarinets.
(Please use a pen on the triplicate forms.)

We'll wash your Toyota to fill up our quota,
We'll clean up your dog or your kids or your yard.
We'd like to be learning, instead we are earning.
(We gladly take checks and all credit cards.)

Friend

Had a friend,
But she turned mean.
Walked around
Like a stuck-up queen.

Nose in the air,
Says she can't play.
Has new friends,
But that's okay.

Remember first grade,
Miss Queen of France?
And the day you wet
Your underpants?

Name Game

His parents call him Jason, but we all call him Weasel,
And David Alexander is better known as Diesel.
Vinnie's name is Popeye, and Mike is Mighty Mouse.
Sam is Spam or Samster, unless we call him House.
Rick is Slick and Dan's the Man and Ted is Freaky Deaky.
But if your name should cause you pain,
Just wait—we change them weekly.

After School

Do you know what happens in the school at night
When the teachers all leave and turn out the light?

The math books count out, "3, 2, 1!"
Then the clock on the wall shouts, "Time for fun!"

The erasers start to race around the floor.
The rubber stamps stamp right out of the drawer.

The scissors cut up, and the stickers peel out.
The paper clips twist, the globe spins about.

The flag waves, "Bye-bye! Don't be late!"
As the wall calendar goes out on a date.

The telephone gives the map a ring.
The ruler gets bossy and acts like a king.

The glue sticks together and the pencils point,
Till the class bell clangs, "Clean up this joint!"

So if something in your desk doesn't look just right,
Maybe it's because of what happened last night.

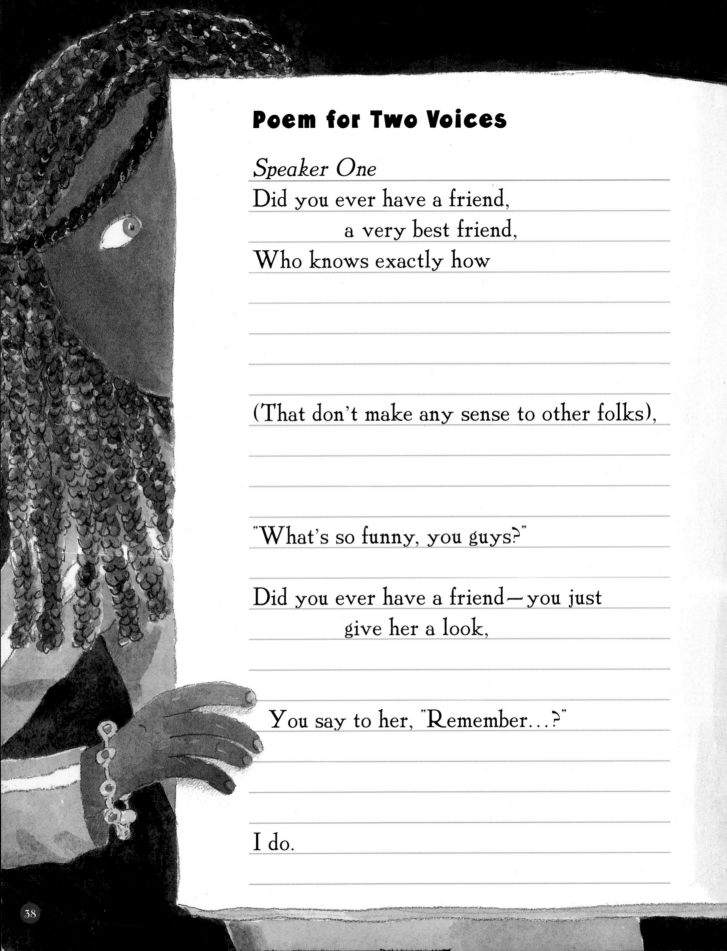

Poem for Two Voices

Speaker One

Did you ever have a friend,
        a very best friend,
Who knows exactly how

(That don't make any sense to other folks),

"What's so funny, you guys?"

Did you ever have a friend—you just
        give her a look,

You say to her, "Remember...?"

I do.

Speaker Two

Your sentences will end?

And the two of you share some goofy,
            silly jokes

But both of you start laughing
            so hard you almost cry,
While other people say,
"What's so funny, you guys?"

And she knows what you are thinking
            like it's written in a book.

And she says, "I totally do."

Did you ever have a friend like that?

Me, too.

Carol Diggory Shields has written books in rhyme about dinosaurs, Martians, insects, fighting food, and American history. Her very favorite subject, however, is school. "School is one of the most fascinating habitats on earth—especially now that I don't HAVE to be there!" The author of many popular picture books, including *I Am Really a Princess* and *Lunch Money and Other Poems About School* (both illustrated by Paul Meisel), Ms. Shields is also the coordinator of children's services for the Salinas Public Library in California. Her husband teaches bilingual kindergarten. She has two college-age sons and a dog that looks like an Ewok.

Paul Meisel attended school for eighteen years and believes it is a good place, even though giving oral reports always made him turn "red as a rose" and feel as though he had forgotten to wear pants. He says that "annoying types" at school sometimes dubbed him "measle," to his dismay. He is the illustrator of many lively books for children, including his own *Zara's Hats*. He lives with his family (which includes three school-age sons) in Newtown, Connecticut.